Smithereens

Smithereens

SHREYA SINGH

PARTRIDGE
A Penguin Company

Partridge books may be ordered through booksellers or by contacting:

Partridge India
Penguin Books India Pvt.Ltd
11, Community Centre, Panchsheel Park, New Delhi 110017
India
www.partridgepublishing.com
Phone: 000.800.10062.62

Contents

To Baba (Mohanji) for always, always being there and for providing me with the strength to aim higher each time. Not one poem in this book would have been possible without his grace.

Shreya Singh is a 17-year-old high school student. She lives in Gurgaon, India and is an avid reader and an enthusiastic writer. Her love for Literature stems from her appreciation of Palahniuk and Murakami novels and the poetry of T.S. Eliot and Andrea Gibson. She wishes to pursue English Literature at college.

Someday we will dare
to write the poems
that will make the world question
whether or not
we are good people.
Someday we will dare
to trade good for true.

—Andrea Gibson
(Poets)

Preface

I began writing at the tender age of seven, when I was admitted in a boarding school far away from home. Books and writing have always been my solace and my safe place. The collection of poems, printed in this book, 'Smithereens,' is one that I have been working on for the past year.

This book wouldn't have been possible without the immense help I received from a long list of people. Firstly, Rita Ma'am, who instilled in me the love for English. Chandreyee Ma'am, for being an absolutely incredible English teacher. My parents and my grandmother for instilling in me the faith that I was capable of achieving this and my sister, Aditi, for always being there and cheering me on. My uncle, Dhanesh Ranjan, for believing in me and assisting me through all the hurdles and for making this a reality. My friends, Anastasia, Diva and Aakriti for always being a pillar of strength. Karnika, for painstakingly helping me title each and every one of the poems in this collection. Karan, for helping me out patiently, when I was indecisive about the title of the book and also for providing me with honest feedback when I needed it the most. Jhanvi, for being my most frank critique and Jasmine, for her tremendous help. Last but definitely not the least, a big thank you to every single member of the Partridge Team who has worked on this with me. The total amount of money gained from the selling of this book will be donated to empower the girl child.

Unoccupied

I want to sleep for a while
Not the kind where your eyelids flutter
Like a dying bird's wings
And you open your eyes
For a moment
Not in your skin.
But the kind
When you sleep so safe and sound
That you forget about your existence
And the stress
And the world
And yourself.
The kind where a dream plays out like an
Oscar winning movie
And where you meet and see people you've never met.

I want to sleep for a long, long while
And wake up in this skin
And body
And look, at my world with sleep drunk eyes.
The kind where you can smell
And lick the morning dew off your arm
Where you can roll down, rough, gravely roads
Without it piercing your back.
I want to go away for a while.
Walk out of this skin, into nothing.
And just be nothing.
Sit on a pavement

And drown into everything.

Saccharine Untruths

I want you to
Lie to me
Everyday. Without fail.
Lie to me so beautifully
That I no longer seek the truth
That is bitter
And too close to reality.
Lie to me so passionately
That I will not need love or hate
Any longer.
Lie to me so calmly
That I will be hypnotized by
The rhythm of your breath
And the call of your letters.
Lie to me so truthfully
So that I forget
That lies even
Exist.

Jigsaw Puzzle

I have tasted the stars
Smelt the moonlight
Felt the soothing thunder
Heard the smiles and tears fall off
In the dark corners of our rooms
And seen the unfairness
That is the string that joins this world together
I have been burnt by the hotness of sunlight
When I tried to taste it
And the blue skies
That look like crystal clear water
Have almost drowned me
I have wondered what it would be like
To stargaze from the moon
Wondered if the sun just takes its makeup off
As it prepares for bed
I have seen beauty
And destruction
And love
And hate
And satisfying joy
And gut wrenching sorrow
And I am still left wondering
Where do I fit in.

Punctured World

A glass bottle
That sits there
Quietly
On an empty table and observes
The world.
The girl with the crooked teeth
And the boy with a heart like a
Superstar's mansion
And the man behind the counter
Wiping glasses
And catching his reflection in the occasional turn
Secretly thinking he looks beautiful
And the woman outside the pub
Walking with a balloon in her hand
That is as fragile as her trust
The chair that sits idle
Waiting to be occupied
So that it doesn't feel useless any more
And the cap of the bottle thrown away

Shreya Singh

In the dustbin in the far corner,
Flirting with the cork.
The bottle looks ahead
Towards the windows for the first time
And sees itself.
It's not pretty.
It doesn't have a heart.
But it just reflects what
It sees around itself.
It wonders if it is real?
Is anything?
It spins
And smashes to the floor
Into bits and pieces as infinite as the stars
And takes its last breath
Finally realizing that everyone
Only lives
Moments before their death.

Stained Humanity

Groping in the dark
And imagining the sun sets in the
West
How will you teach that little boy
That love only exists in dingy corners of the world
Where the sun forgets to shine sometimes
How will you tell him that life
Is a stadium
That is burning slowly and steadily
How will you teach him to look up at the sky
Without spotting the remnants of smoke.
In what way will you communicate to him
That sometimes people will light his feelings like a
Cigarette and throw it away, when it'll make them cough.
How will you teach him that having emotions
In this desperate desperate race
Is like being stabbed over and over again
By your most precious pen.
When we look out into this world
And see through our fists
And turn a blind eye to the damaged canvas
That lies soaking wet in your room
Will you be able to point out
Into this earth and demonstrate what hope is?
What will you show him after everything has been destroyed
While he is stumbling in the dark
That makes him want to fly
And still call this place
Home.

Hooded Guise

In the dead of the night
as we sit on the hood of
your car
and look out into the world
I wonder how everything is
just nothing in disguise
And then I turn towards you
and ask
what colour your car is.

Absolut Undress

Warm liquid travels down your
throat
drips down your chin
and gets lost
underneath your shirt.
I watch the stream disappear
and for a split second
catch my reflection in the drop of alcohol before it
wanders out of sight.
I see myself then,
drinking
and immediately spitting out
life.

Snivelling Silence

Wailing in the night
I saw a child who was left to die on the pavement
He looked at me with his dark pain drunk eyes
And asked me
Why the world was such a cruel place
I smiled
Walked by him
He held my hand
Repeated his question
And I smiled wider
Looked up at the sky
But there weren't any stars
Only disfigured cold stones
Wrapped in
A silver foil.

Vagrant Moods

Growling in thin air
Shaking the bed sheet
off her shoulders
she wondered
if love
is a bruise
that fades away
with time
or if it
is a pair
of slippers
that tear and
lose each other as
time goes by.
As the bed sheet
fell to the ground
and she inhaled the
moonlight
and saw the lights
shine in the
run down houses
she knew
that love
was instead
a homeless person
who slept on
the park bench
each
night.

Rise

The silver twilight touches your skin,
And the sound of waves crashing against the earthly soil,
dances in your ears.
The grass that you rest on, stands higher as if to peek into
distant, long forgotten lands,
As the crepuscular light is shown through the silhouette of
the big bushes.
The dark black sky that looks upon you is as clear as the tear
that blooms often and balances at the tip of your eyelash.
And the cool wind, whips across your face and runs through
your hair like a never stopping traveler on a mission.
The pureness of the moment touches you and then fades away.
Moments are like magic. They never stay long enough for
you to decipher its true essence.
Close your eyes and in your mind's eye, get lost in darkness.
Construct things in darkness and feel in the darkness, let it
pour into you and taste it on your tongue.
Build a world in darkness; because you'll often fall into it
And no one but darkness can be your guide through the dark.
You'll touch time today; it's a secret that you shall never tell.
You'll smell it in the soil by the beach,
And see it in the midnight sky.
You'll see it leaving, through the little holes in the bushes,
And pass along with the rushing wind.
And you'll sense its light caress, as you walk through the dark.
Sigh. And let it mingle with the scene around you.
And smile, because no one else exists.
The world, lies at your jaded feet.
So rise and embrace it.

Stricken

There is something that you should know,
The secret that lurks behind your black eyes,
The cry that hides behind your pink lips,
The shyness that peaks from your lowered eyelash
And the electricity that flows through your long tresses.

The creamy skin pooled underneath the tightened bow,
The night that falls on your cheeks and the moon that looks upon the pureness of your soul.
The cascading winds that clash with the electrifying hair and the birds those now fly out to their nests.
The little grasshoppers that are illuminated by the moonlight
And the reflection of you on the white gleaming floor.

Beauty destroys mind and soul.
You want to cave it within the boundaries to save it before it fades out.
It lurks in your eyes today.
I can hear the silent cry for help.
I can see the boldness that wishes to come to light,
And the electricity that is soon dying out.

But I can do no such thing,
For I am nothing but the reflection that you see each day in the mirror.
I fade.

Effortless Slumber

You asked me once
if I sleep to dream
or to escape this world
I had smiled at you then
a smile
that conveyed nothing more
or less
than a smile
but I can tell you
now
that I sleep
to feel and then
forget
because that can't be achieved
so easily
if we are
awake.

Burnt Spectacle

Touching the coarseness of his mouth
Was like swimming in a pool
Full of jagged stones.
Reckless.
Frightening.
Exhilarating.
Feeling the rough jab of his fingers
On my waist was crushing
It woke me
Up into another world
Where everything existed.
Not like this one
Where only some things do.
I couldn't take out a map
Feel its glossy surface
And point out to where this place was.
It was like closing your eyes and shaking your
Head fast and hard.
It felt like
A person does when they come undone.
Utterly.
Completely.
And feel parts of them fly to places
They have never even been to.
His breath in my face
Was like smoke
That I inhaled
Leaving me to wonder
If it would soon turn into
A fire
And burn all that I am.

Another Realm

Can we float
away
from this world.
It has too much beauty
And too much hate.
And too much love.
That the world itself
Can't bear.
So if we float
away
today
Maybe we'll make
its load
lighter.
And you and I can
float
into another world
and look at this one
from

afar.

Sinister Corner

I can see regret leaking
from your eyes
tonight
I can sense the words
that lap and thrash
in
this distance between us
only to drown
I can feel the
ground
detaching itself from
the world
for a moment,
as you wipe the regret
and today
your eyes are not
a mirror to
your soul
but just eyes
that help you see
tonight
what you have made of me.

For Salma (12th June 2013)

She was a little girl
Her voice mixed perfectly with the wind
And her shiny braid
Fell seamlessly down her back
Washed in sunshine
She was shy and quiet
And didn't know that the world existed in her eyes
That her mind was softer and purer than a white rose
And her thoughts a beautiful chain
I could wear all day around my neck.
But then she went
And she no longer exists
And it's so hard
To grasp the fact that I'll never be able to hear or
Touch her again
It's so painful to see death kiss someone and then take
them away
It's heartbreaking
And surprising
And so disgusting.
It's times like these I wish
That death turn into a person
And die slowly and painfully.

Time Machine

When we grow
up and apart
will you
build a
time machine with me
and travel
back to this
very moment
when we lay
on the grass
and gazed at
the sky
which was so
clear
that we could see
through it
and find
the devil trespassing
into
heaven.

Grinded Wits

Crumbled leaves like cake crumbs
Fluttering inside my head
Fighting
And lashing
Asking one another
What the world outside looks like
They tell themselves that they
Are the only ones who can fly
In this world without wings.
But they are crushed
And my mind is the terrain
Where they rest to die.

Distinct Crafting

Even the wind becomes lazy during
the summer evenings
and it rolls and gallops in the sun's rays
and then walks by scrutinizing us
we think everything in the world is made for us
the skies
the sun
the wind
the rain
but what if we were
made for them
after all
we too make their lives as difficult and smooth
as they make ours
what if we weren't made for ourselves at all
but for everything around us.

Vacant Recall

Knock.
Punch.
Clap.
Give up
on me
this moment
that lies
empty
between our feet
like a licked
vanilla ice-cream cup
screeches
as you step on
it
and realise
that you
now
like
a different
flavour.

Untitled

Are the gaps between your teeth
a symbol for the words
that escaped the prison of your mind?

Are the scars on your arm
a symbol for the feelings that
disentangled from your caged heart
only to fly out like a free bird?

Are the bags under your eyes
a symbol for the heavy luggage
squashing the pavement of hope in your
head?

Are you a symbol for the world that exists

Until it doesn't.

Uninvited

She fell on her knees
Tasted the robes
Squeezed the towel
And petted the vase.
There was a party in her mind tonight
And she didn't know the cause for celebration
She took each breath
Not as if it were her last
But first.
Did she find breathing unfamiliar
When she did it first?
That's how she felt.
Unknown.
Lost.
She was the window reflecting back
The wrecked room.
She was the phone that lay strewn on
The carpeted floor.
She wondered when this merry making would end.
When the guests would all leave
And allow her
Her peace.
She waited
Until she felt one with the clock on
The cracked wall.
Until the music in her brain came to a halt.
They weren't going anywhere.
Just sleeping over for the night.

Amma

She was like a town
That no matter how old
Remains ageless and beautiful.
Her eyes were the streets
where thoughts, questions
and love
lived side by side.
Her words the serene park
that dragged everyone in.
I'd go there often
and sit
look at the roads, houses and the grass
strung together so perfectly.
Days passed
And a violent storm struck
Nearly destroying everything
But she stood back up again and
Swallowed the pain quietly.

The town is still there
She is still there
But there's just no way
To get there anymore.

Submerge

Flying slowly
Casually wandering
Upwards
Towards the sun hoping
To crash and burn
I made my heart the island
Where the parachute of your
Sweet salty words would land
And my mouth the town
Where I wanted to keep you trapped
Forever.
But by the time you flew up
Steadily to the sky
There was no sun
Only the moon
And there you setup a house
Made out of moonlight
Then my island drowned
And the town broke down
Into pieces
That now only look beautiful
Bathed in the moon's shine.
Bathed in you.

Shards of Time

Will you break
time
into small fragments
that no one can join back
and I
will take a needle
and try
to sew it back together
But I can't.
So don't break
time.

One Common Thing

If you die once
You don't have to
die
Again.
The world will spin
Chaos will reign
Hearts will shatter
Like a piece
of glass that splinters
when time twirls
it the wrong
way in its dance.
Moments will rise
Hatred will rule
And the devil
will take long walks
in the park.
But you
You will be
dead
And still wonder
how each one
of us doesn't have life
in common
but Death.

Blemished Reflection

Look at me through
a broken glass
and I'll make a whole image
joined at the edges by cracks
you'll see me clearly then
look into my imperfections
like a new-born fish exploring the sea
but you won't run
because it will be just an image
and not the real me.

Aching Animosity

He woke up
each day
wanting to be great
wondering
what no one had
thought of before
So that he could
change the world
what is the
one thing
he could do
to alter everything
in the blink of an eye
He was a
little boy.
Thought if he
sharpened his pencils properly
and threw away the
shavings
Peace would reign
But now
he is twenty-three
and he sits on
the window-pain
and

gazes at the
silent night
while miles away
wars rage and
people die
And he thinks
how that
one person survived
who first felt
hatred.

The Tempest

Deep inside you
somewhere today there's a
storm brewing
it's rising like bile
in your throat
and building a city in your mouth
storms destroy towns, yes.
But this one's building it
Constructing it piece by piece
Rising up
Like hidden desires that wander like
Ghosts in the chambers of your mind
There's a storm building a city in
You tonight
And your soul
Is eagerly witnessing it through the gates
Patiently, waiting to take residence.

Pale Heart

Tattered inside
My heart is made of paper
That is yellowed at the edges
And has holes
No blood
No soul
Just ink
That has faded
Like the ugly moon in the sky
Which looked like a rounded tooth
In your rosy mouth
That spat out blood
That was as red as the blush
On her cheeks
The night you
Ate up all the stars
And tore through
My yellowed heart.

Moon Crumbs

You were the half eaten sandwich
That lay rotten on my bed sheet
For days
The smell of your
Devious onion
Took over my room
And the slimy
Cheese
Became one with

I found you
Tangled up in my bed
And I brushed the tiny crumbs
That stuck like magnets to
The now yellowing whiteness of my
Heaven
But you were everywhere
Your smell
Your taste
Your existence
I slept in it each night
Until one day I smelt like you
And threw you out
But you flew up and
Became one with the stars
And the moon welcomed you with
Open arms

And you now look upon me every night
Bathing the yellowed sheet
In you
One with the moon
A part of me
Forever.

Free Fall

Fall into yourself
tonight
fall so hard and fast that
you don't get to see what's really
inside you
because if you do see
then there's no way out
you're stuck with you
for the rest of your life
the only way out
is to fall in love
and fall deep inside someone else
but not too deep because
you'll be stuck.
So it's best to descend into yourself
because even though we never express it
we all
secretly love ourselves the most.

Pint of Gloom

You can pour sadness in a cup
at two am
and I'll drink it carefully
as if it were
the last cup.
I'll sip it and taste it
and allow it to
melt into my being.
I'll drink it.
Sadness.
I'll nurse that cup throughout the
night
And when it's empty
I'll cry
and beg for more.
But you must
push me
towards
the first door
that points to
where
I can take all
This sadness out.

Rootless Breeze

What is it about dark nights
That unhinge the other side of us
My mind turns into a deserted playground
Where a wandering wind rests
Then sleepwalks and
Plucks out the grass
Eating it
Hoping it smells as fresh.

Blind Mirror

Looking through a mirror
I see you.
Siting there
perfectly.
Still.
Like a pure river,
unmoving.
Like a dead body.
Dark.
Like the night that
covers your insides
where your soul
resides.
Looking through a mirror
I see
me.
Watching you.
Watching me.

First Whistle

Flames like
That of a fire that rages
And kills
Not people
But their hearts
And you jumped headfirst
To escape me
While I stood on the side-lines
Like a spectator at a
Football game that has not yet
Begun
While the players stand in position on the field
But you never came out
I saw you burn
And I didn't move
Because the whistle
Hadn't yet been blown
To signal the start of the
Game.

Recess

Knock at night.
Ask life where it
has been all this while
and
why it has appeared now
at your doorstep
while the world sleeps
and you sweat through
your shirt
it offers you a drink
and you invite it in.
Take out the snow.
Dust your shoes.
Blow out the candles.
And stab this cigarette
In the ashtray
of your heart.

Worthless Trinket

I was the coin
you stored away in
your purse
never using it
keeping it
holding it
praying you never
lose it
asking me
which shop
would accept me
and fling me into
the air
tie me with a
parachute
and you glance slowly
at the items
stored at the back
of the aisle
Deposit me
beside a
milk container
and disappear
for
a while.

Splinters of Dust

Falling at your feet
like fragments of dust
you looked like an
unblemished moon
with your eyes as endless as deserts
and your mouth
as perfect as the rest of you.
I fell.
I was scattered
at your feet.
But when I looked
up
your face was
a raging, violent
unrecognizable
sun.

Black Ice

You are like a
Haunted house
I was scared to enter at first
The look of you
Thrilled my
Veins
And froze my brain
Into a large ice cube
That can't fit into any ice tray
But I took a deep breath
And took a step into the
World that was you
Scary and
Deathly
I closed my eyes
Inside you
It was as dark as the sun
That had drawn its curtains
Too
Angry at the world
For being so breathtakingly beautiful
But when I opened them
And touched the gravely surface
Of your inner walls and sat by the piano
That played the songs that roamed like strangers in your heart

I was happy.
Haunted.
Dead.
Locked.
And so in love
With your black
black
Dark.

Crash and Burn

Falling at your feet
Like unused letters
The words flew out
From the cages of my mouth
Only to crash
On your shoes
They broke
Into a million pieces
And you brushed them off
Like dust
And walked ahead
Into this oblivious and knowing world
Not knowing
That some were still stuck
To the soul of your shoe.

Fumbling Anarchy

Chaos.
Swirls and froths in
me
it lingers and waits
like the moon's
gentle imprint in the
early morning sky
it leaps and runs
in circles
like a cat chasing
a mouse
it chases my beliefs
it squashes my soul
it sits on it for a long, long time
until it is the blood
running through
my veins
chaos is the mentor
that holds my hand and leads
me
to
reality.

Dense Echo

I love the sound
of a stone dropping
into a pot of water.
The sound is so thick
that I can fold my
whole life and fit it
between
it.
It is so deep,
that I can fit anything
that belongs to me in it.
And sail away
just for that one second.
One second.
Plop.

A Bottle, A Song

He drank.
Tasted the mouth of the bottle
And let it rub against his rubbery lips
He allowed it to flow through him
His insides the holy site
Where the holy river flowed
He looked around
Saw the world
Felt disgusted
And took a swig again.
Tapped his feet
To a long forgotten song
That his father sang to him every night
Until he was shot
In the mouth
And when the rim touched his slippery cave
He wondered
If his lips looked
Just like his
Father's.

Barren World

She sipped
coffee
feeling it slither down
her throat like a
snake
Crawling out from its resting
place.
Her insides became the
jungle
That is wild
and green
and deadly
Each breath she let
out
A fire
Each breath she took
in
water.
And she set down
her cup.
Traced the curve of
her cheek.
And prayed
for the forest
to turn into
an
abandoned town.

Stray Debris

I was the paper
You were the envelope
And I folded myself perfectly
So I could fit inside you
Our love was the glue
That kept us together
But then time passed
And the glue dried
You opened yourself
As if inviting other papers in
I was thrown out onto the dark dark table
Days passed
And I saw you do the same with so many other papers
Until one day you came back
The glue in your hand
Asking for me again
But it was too late
Because I had grown too much
To fit back into you.

Rainbow Stains

My body is a
dark movie theatre
that lies
empty
most of the time
But
when you
come by
once in a while
because you're bored
my body becomes
a
circus.

Will You

Will you wrap me around your stillness
And allow me to float through your mind
My heart is a puddle you step on each day
And my tears the rain, you dance in every time.

Stifling Disclosure

You can close your eyes,
Unfold your palms
And carry my whole world in it.
You can curl them then
And squeeze it tight
And strangle me,
With it.

Unread

You were a book
I couldn't open
And couldn't read
Just fingered the spine
Memorized the synopsis
And gasped through
The end.

Cake Box

That mountain is
A piece of cake
The white clouds above it
The white icing
The twinkling stars are the glowing candles
While the navy blue sky, the cake box
Us?
We are just crumbs.

Pulp Feast

Flesh on flesh
Like a sandwich of your soul
That god will devour on tonight
And lick his fingers,
Brush off the crumbs
And allow a small tiny piece of your spirit
Slip by him on the plate
To remind you
That the world is not as kind.

Flash Destruction

Flash in front of my eyes
Trail like a wind
In the busy streets of my mind
Break the walls
I constructed so painstakingly
In my heart and lounge on the furniture you
See beyond it
Crawl like an unhappy child
In my thoughts
And throw the camera
When the reel runs out.

Memory Food

Like a framed photograph
She framed this moment
And put it
In her stomach
Hoping that when
The time was right
Her body
Would flush
it
Out.

Whole-Halves

I was like a
Half done dish
Served cold
On a dirty table cloth
With a bent spoon
While you were the crooked
Wine glass that fell
On top of me
By accident and
Made me whole.